CARVING ORNAMENTAL MINIATURE FLYING BIRDS

With Patterns and Instructions for 16 Projects

by Anthony Hillman

DOVER PUBLICATIONS, INC., New York

Copyright © 1991 by Anthony Hillman.
All rights reserved under Pan American and International Copyright Conventions.

Published in Canada by General Publishing Company, Ltd., 30 Lesmill Road, Don Mills, Toronto, Ontario.
Published in the United Kingdom by Constable and Company, Ltd., 3 The Lanchesters, 162–164 Fulham Palace Road, London W6 9ER.

Carving Ornamental Miniature Flying Birds: With Patterns and Instructions for 16 Projects is a new work, first published by Dover Publications, Inc., in 1991. These patterns and drawings are not to be used for printed reproduction without permission.

Manufactured in the United States of America
Dover Publications, Inc., 31 East 2nd Street, Mineola, N.Y. 11501

Library of Congress Cataloging-in-Publication Data

Hillman, Anthony.
    Carving ornamental miniature flying birds : with patterns and instructions
        for 16 projects / by Anthony Hillman.
            p.   cm.
        ISBN 0-486-26726-1 (pbk.)
        1. Wood-carving. 2. Wood-carving—Patterns. 3. Miniature craft. 4. Birds in
            art. I. Title.
TT199.7.H545   1991
731.4'62—dc20
                                                                                    91-2262
                                                                                    CIP

How to Carve an Ornamental Miniature Flying Bird

Miniature bird carvings have their advantages: a minimal amount of wood is required to produce extremely fine carvings that occupy very little space. Miniature ornamental carvings that can be displayed by hanging require even less room. They are particularly welcome when you have run out of shelf space, and they also make colorful, attractive ornaments that may be hung in windows, on Christmas trees and elsewhere. The sixteen bird carvings that can be made from the patterns in this book represent some of America's most colorful and best-known songbirds and hummingbirds. In fact there is no state of the United States or province of Canada where at least one of these birds—usually more—may not be seen at least part of the year.

To begin, select the patterns for the bird you wish to carve and cut that page free. (All the pattern pages may be removed at once if you wish by extracting the staples.) The paper on which the patterns are printed is heavy enough to provide excellent templates, but if you plan on reusing the templates several times, you may wish to glue them to cardboard or thin plywood. If this is done, recut the templates and apply a thin coat of varnish to seal the edges.

Note: *Only the profile and top-view patterns are to be used as templates. Do not mount the front-view patterns!* These are for reference only.

For each carving I have given the dimensions of the wood stock required. When in doubt it is always a good idea to use pieces that are a little larger; these can always be cut down if necessary.

When you cut out the shape in the wood it is very important to consider the direction of the wood grain. The grain should always run along the length of the top surface of the tail. In the pieces for the wings, which should be cut out separately (more on this later), the grain should always run in the same direction as the outermost primary flight feather (see Figure 1).

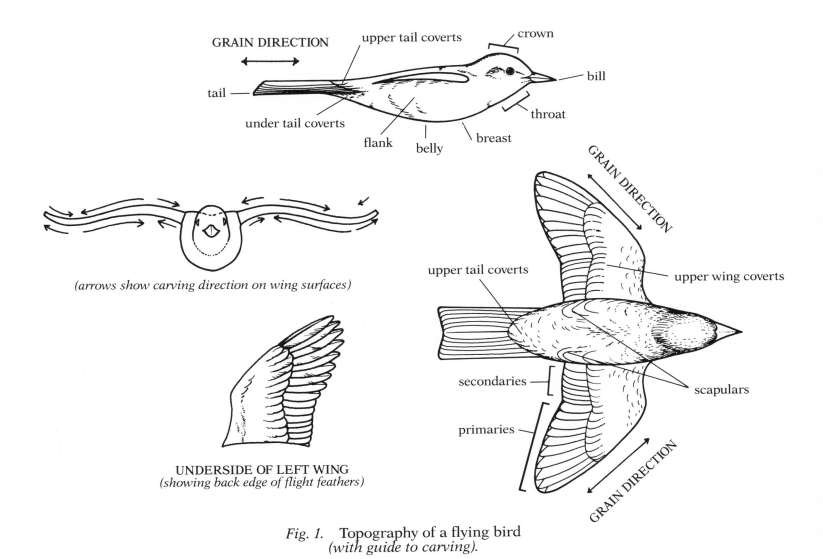

Fig. 1. Topography of a flying bird
(with guide to carving).

Selecting the Wood

Basswood (linden) is by far the most popular wood for carving miniatures, with clear-grained white pine running a close second. There are many mail-order suppliers of carving woods, and booths where supplies are sold may be found at most of the larger bird-carving shows.

Experiment with softwoods available in your own region, since a local source is usually much more economical and convenient. Several dollars' worth of quality wood will provide enough material for many, many miniature bird carvings.

Getting Started: Carving a Flying Robin

An American Robin makes a good first project. Among the most familiar songbirds, robins are found throughout the United States and Canada, often intently foraging for worms and insects on lawns and in open woodlands.

To start, cut out the profile and top-view templates. (The robin's tail is cut out with the body. For the two hummingbirds, the tail may be cut out separately and inserted into the body. This procedure is not recommended for beginners.) Except for the Rose-breasted Grosbeak, the top-view templates for the carvings in this book include the wings. Although it is advisable to leave these attached on the templates for convenience, the wings and body should be cut out separately. To be able to do this, cut a slot between each wing and the body on the template, but not all the way through to the front and back edges of each wing (see Fig. 2). The slot should follow the curve that marks the joining of wing and body. Also, cut out the space on the profile template that marks where the wing will be glued on. Now, using an ordinary lead pencil, trace the outline of the profile onto the block of wood. It is a good idea to mark the position of the eyes with a sharp point at this time. Remember that the grain of the wood should run the same way as the tail.

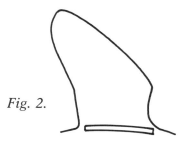

Fig. 2.

You are ready to cut out the profile. This may be done by machine—with a band saw or jigsaw—or by hand, using a coping saw (the safest way). If using a power saw, be sure that there is a sufficient border of wood between the outline and the edge of the wood, or you may cut your fingers. This is a good time to drill holes for the eyes if you are using glass eyes. If you have access to a drill press you can drill a very small hole completely through the head. If you drill separate holes, the usual method with a hand drill, be sure that they are precisely opposite each other, or you will ruin the appearance of your carving. I usually do not use glass eyes on miniature carvings, however. More on this later.

The best way I have found for cutting out the top-view pattern is as follows. Save the top and bottom pieces left over when you have cut out the profile and put them back in place. Secure them with pieces of masking tape or a little rubber cement near the corners. Trace the top-view template onto the top of this (centering it very carefully) and cut out the top-view shape. Finally, carefully draw a line in the exact center of the sawed-out piece on top and bottom, going all the way around (see Fig. 3). This centerline is your guide to symmetrical carving. *Do not cut it away!* The centerline should always remain in place until you give your carving its final sanding.

centerline

Fig. 3.   marked position of wing joint

Before you proceed to carve the body, saw out and carve the wings. When you position the wing templates on the pieces of wood, remember that the direction of the grain must run along the outer primary flight feather (see Fig. 1). *This is very important!* Trace and saw out the wings. Trace the shape of the base of the wing onto the wood on that side using the slot in the profile template. Now refer to the front-view reference pattern and carve the curves on the thickness of the wings. Use Fig. 1 as a guide to the direction of the blade. If you prefer you may saw these curves using a jigsaw or band saw. If you do this, avoid cutting your fingers by holding the wood in a "sandwich" of two thicker pieces of wood. Use sandpaper to refine the curves until the wings are shaped like those in the front-view pattern. Actually the front-view patterns show the wings thicker at the tips than they should end up (I have done this to provide a reference for sawing). You should ultimately carve and sand the wingtips down to a fine feathered edge (see Fig. 4).

Fig. 4.

Next check the fit of the wings to the body. If the wings are not precisely flush with the body, sand them down by using a piece of #120 sandpaper. Fold this over, hold it against the body on each wing joint and rub the base of the wing against the sandpaper, back and forth. If the body itself needs sanding at the wing joints, fold a piece of sandpaper over each wing at the base and use it as a sanding block. Soon you will find that a perfect fit can be obtained.

Now that you have smoothed the wing joints flush, use the base of the wings as templates to trace the outline of the wing joints onto the body. Check your wings. They should both look the same; that is, one should be like a mirror image of the other. They should be equally thick and tapered alike. Otherwise they will differ in weight and your carving will hang lopsided.

When you are satisfied with the shape and thickness of the wings, take a pencil and, using the top-view pattern as a guide, outline the individual feathers and feather groups. Start with the upper wing coverts, then proceed

(Instructions continue after Plates.)

NORTHERN CARDINAL

State bird of seven states, the Northern Cardinal is popular wherever it is found.

PROFILE

Dimensions of Wood Stock:
Body: 4¼″ long × 1¼″ high × 1″ wide
Wings (2 pieces): 2¾″ long × 1¾″ wide ×
   ¾″ thick

Eyes: 3mm black
Actual length of live bird: 8¾″

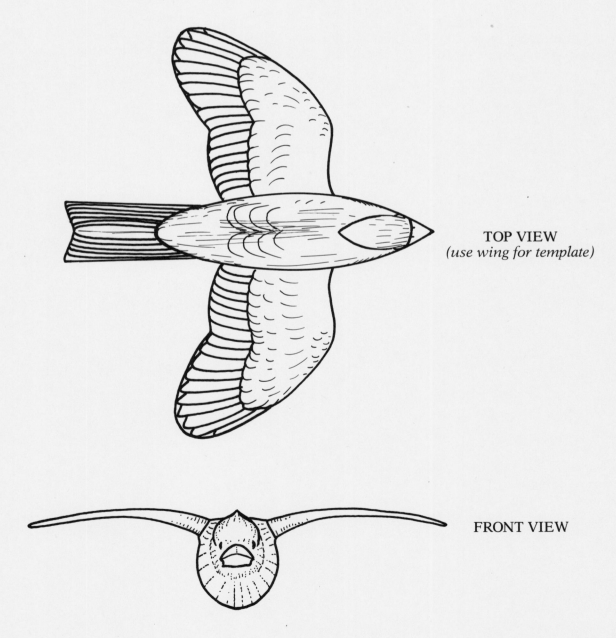

TOP VIEW
(use wing for template)

FRONT VIEW

Plate 1

BLUE JAY

The brightly colored, raucous Blue Jay is one of the most familiar birds in the East.

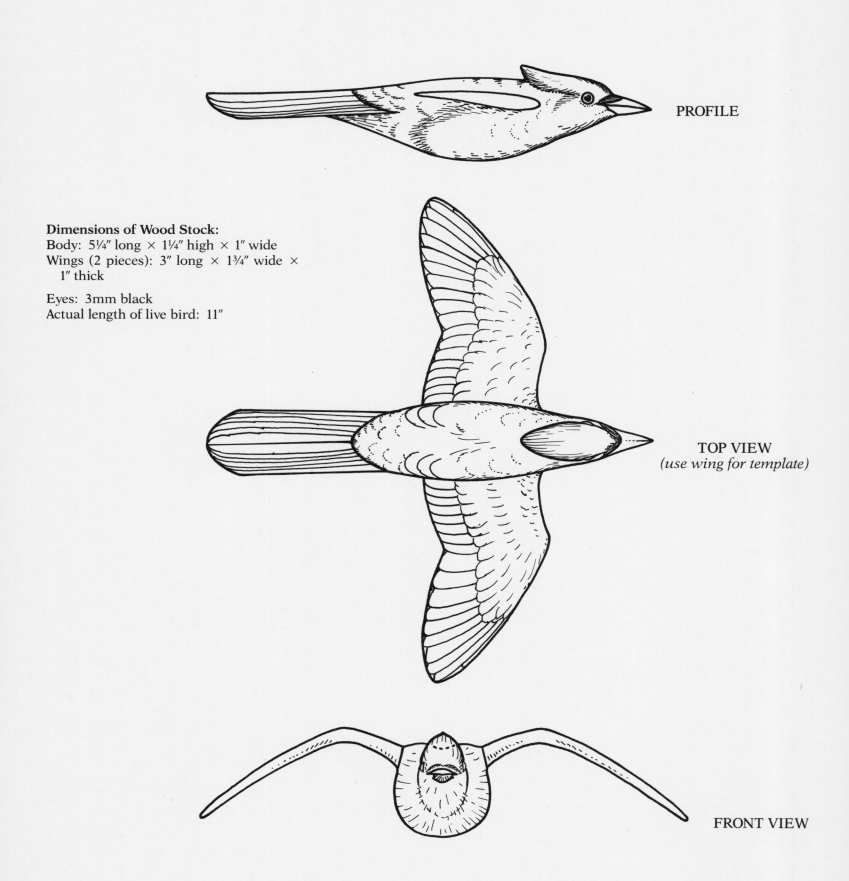

PROFILE

Dimensions of Wood Stock:
Body: 5¼″ long × 1¼″ high × 1″ wide
Wings (2 pieces): 3″ long × 1¾″ wide ×
   1″ thick

Eyes: 3mm black
Actual length of live bird: 11″

TOP VIEW
(use wing for template)

FRONT VIEW

Plate 2

PROTHONOTARY WARBLER

This is one of the most beautiful of the warblers— and unusual,
in its practice of nesting in holes in trees near water.

PROFILE

Dimensions of Wood Stock:
Body: 3¾″ long × 1″ high × 1″ wide
Wings (2 pieces): 2½″ long × 1½″ wide ×
   ½″ thick

Eyes: 2 or 3mm brown or black
Actual length of live bird: 5½″

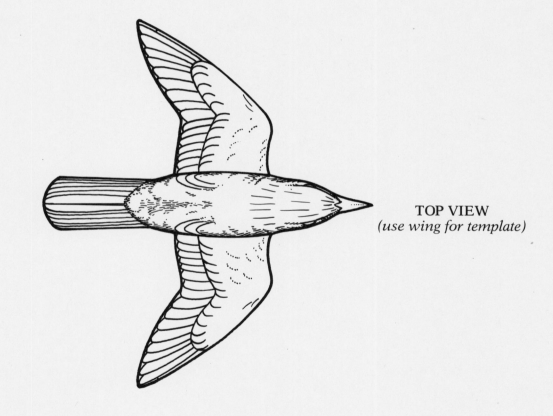

TOP VIEW
(use wing for template)

FRONT VIEW

Plate 3

AMERICAN GOLDFINCH

In the summer this perky seedeater is dazzling in its brilliant yellow-and-black plumage.

PROFILE

Dimensions of Wood Stock:
Body: 3¾″ long × 1¼″ high × 1″ wide
Wings (2 pieces): 2¼″ long × 1¼″ wide ×
 ½″ thick

Eyes: 3mm black or dark brown
Actual length of live bird: 5″

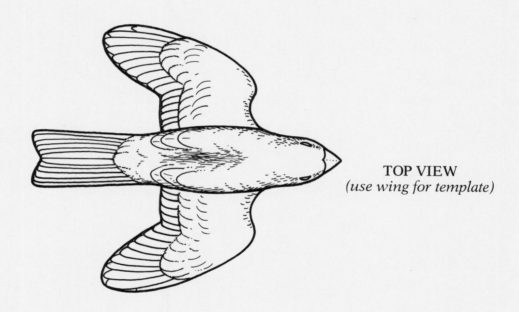

TOP VIEW
(use wing for template)

FRONT VIEW

Plate 4

EASTERN BLUEBIRD

Always admired for its rare beauty, this favorite Eastern thrush is successfully being helped by nest-box programs in the United States and Canada.

PROFILE

Dimensions of Wood Stock:
Body: 4″ long × 1¼″ high × 1″ wide
Wings (2 pieces): 2¾″ long × 1¾″ wide ×
   1″ thick

Eyes: 3mm brown
Actual length of live bird: 7″

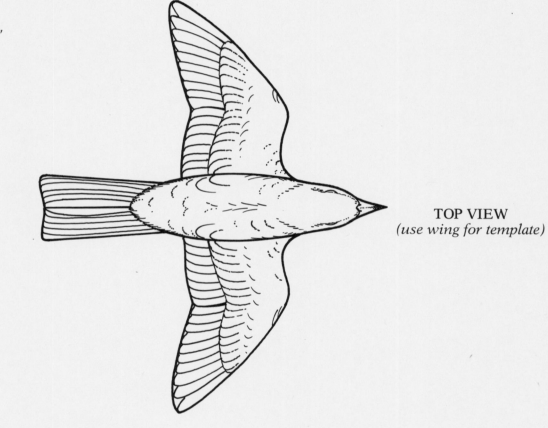

TOP VIEW
(use wing for template)

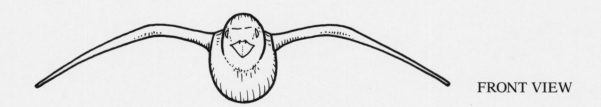

FRONT VIEW

Plate 5

AMERICAN ROBIN

*This is "the early bird that catches the worm"—
on lawns and meadows almost everywhere in North America.*

PROFILE

Dimensions of Wood Stock:
Body: 4¾″ long × 1½″ high × 1¼″ wide
Wings (2 pieces): 3″ long × 1¾″ wide ×
 ¾″ thick

Eyes: 3mm dark brown
Actual length of live bird: 10″

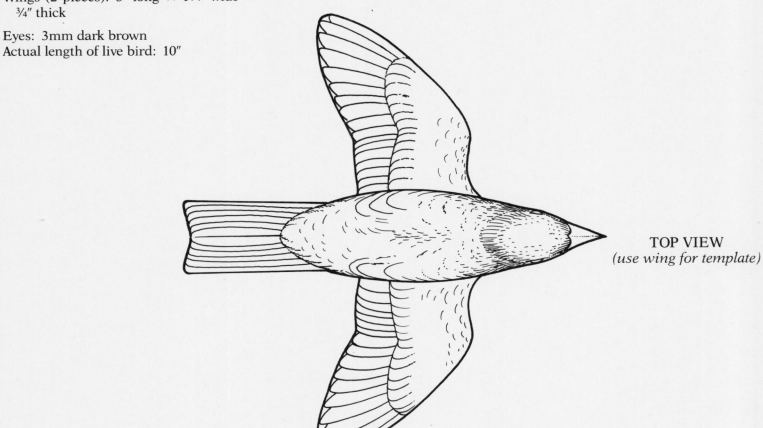

TOP VIEW
(use wing for template)

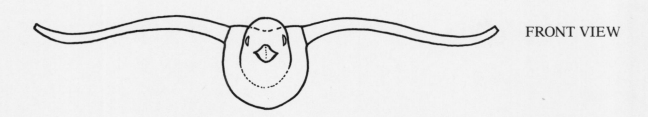

FRONT VIEW

Plate 6

BLACK-CAPPED CHICKADEE

The Black-capped Chickadee is one of the best-known woodland birds, found throughout most of the northern United States and much of Canada.

PROFILE

Dimensions of Wood Stock:
Body: 4″ long × 1¼″ high × 1¼″ wide
Wings (2 pieces): 2½″ long × 1½″ wide × ½″ thick

Eyes: 3mm black or dark brown
Actual length of live bird: 5¼″

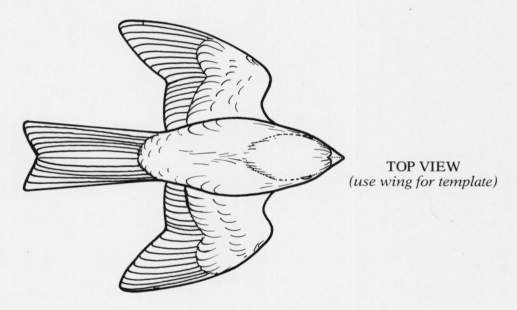

TOP VIEW
(use wing for template)

FRONT VIEW

Plate 7

WESTERN TANAGER

Seen only in the West, the Western Tanager is one of the most brilliant of a primarily tropical bright-plumaged family of birds.

PROFILE

Dimensions of Wood Stock:
Body: 4¼″ long × 1¼″ high × 1¼″ wide
Wings (2 pieces): 2½″ long × 1½″ wide × ½″ thick

Eyes: 3mm black or dark brown
Actual length of live bird: 7¼″

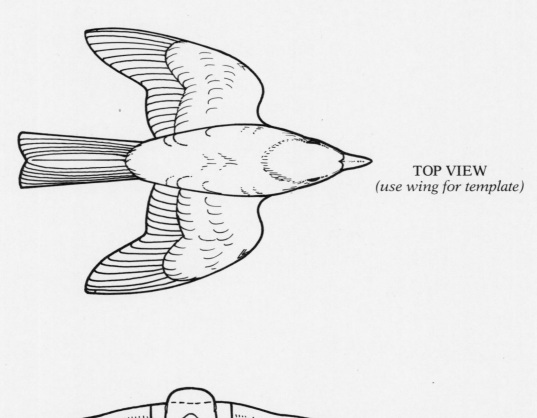

TOP VIEW
(use wing for template)

FRONT VIEW

Plate 8

PAINTED BUNTING

*Actually a sparrow, the strikingly colored Painted Bunting
at first view looks nothing like its drabber cousins.*

PROFILE

Dimensions of Wood Stock:
Body: 4″ long × 1½″ high × 1½″ wide
Wings (2 pieces): 2½″ long × 1¾″ wide ×
   1″ thick

Eyes: 3mm dark brown or black
Actual length of live bird: 5¼″

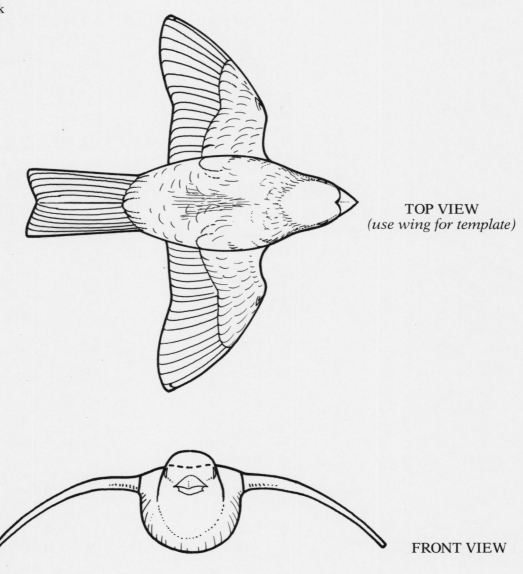

TOP VIEW
(use wing for template)

FRONT VIEW

Plate 9

RED-WINGED BLACKBIRD

A familiar bird of wetlands and fields throughout North America.

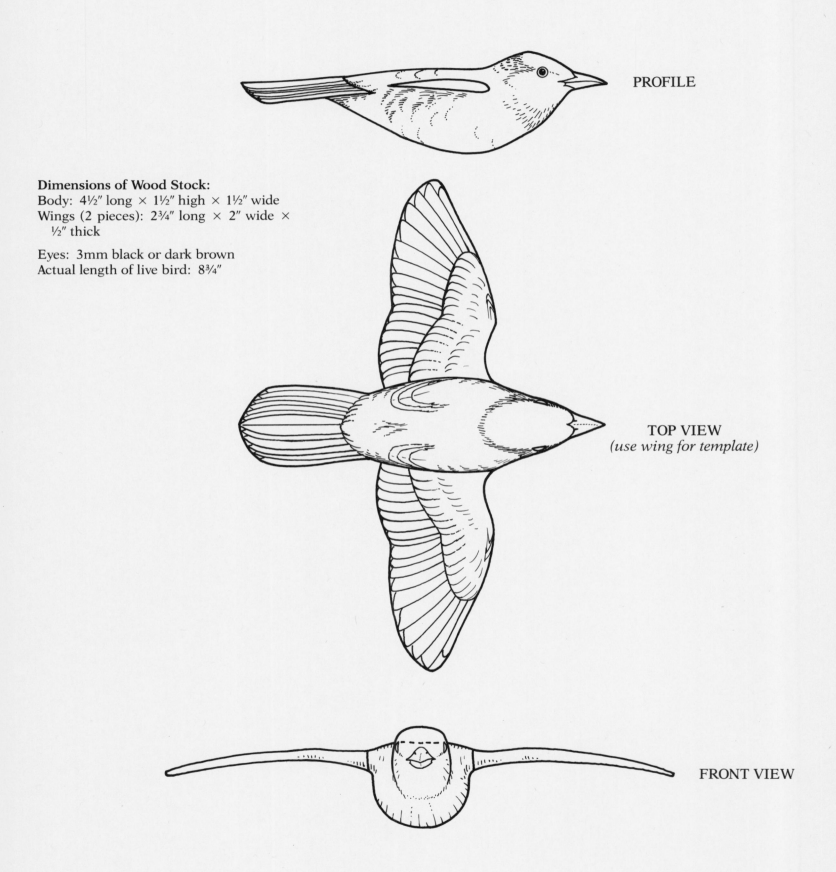

PROFILE

Dimensions of Wood Stock:
Body: 4½″ long × 1½″ high × 1½″ wide
Wings (2 pieces): 2¾″ long × 2″ wide ×
    ½″ thick

Eyes: 3mm black or dark brown
Actual length of live bird: 8¾″

TOP VIEW
(use wing for template)

FRONT VIEW

Plate 10

WOOD THRUSH

A common but not always easy-to-see spot-breasted thrush of the East, the Wood Thrush delights hikers and residents of the forest with its haunting song.

PROFILE
(use wing for template)

Dimensions of Wood Stock:
Body: 3¾″ long × 1½″ high × 1¼″ wide
Wings (2 pieces): 2½″ long × 1¾″ wide ×
    ½″ thick

Eyes: 3mm dark brown
Actual length of live bird: 7¾″

TOP VIEW
(use as body template)

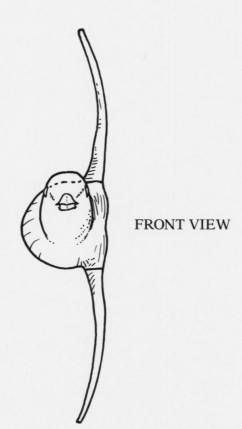

FRONT VIEW

Plate 11

ROSE-BREASTED GROSBEAK

A relative of the more familiar cardinal, the Rose-breasted Grosbeak is also an Eastern bird but seen only in the warmer months, for it winters in the tropics.

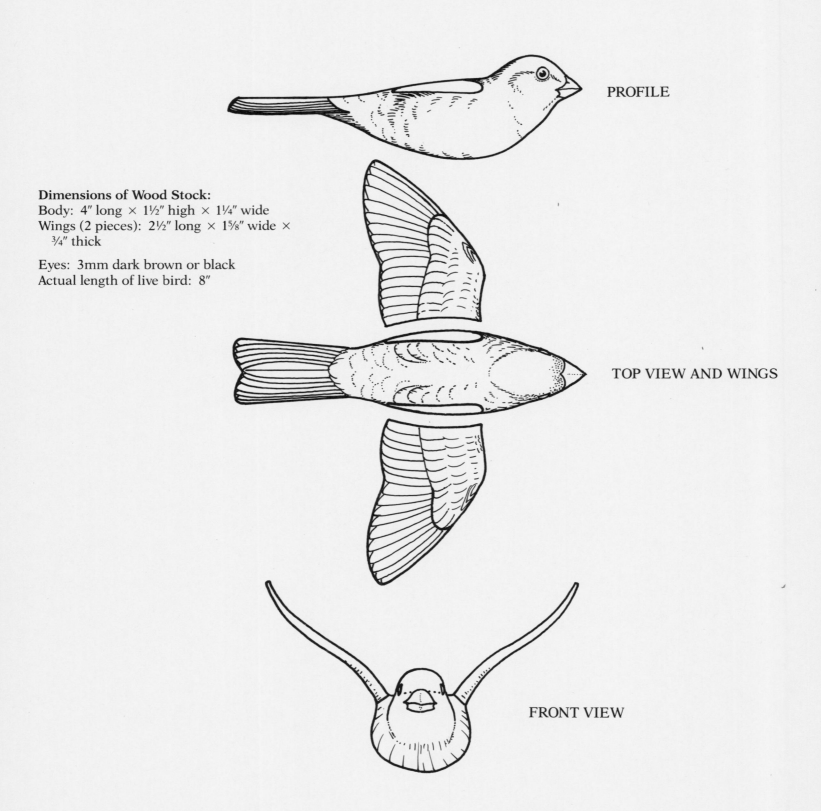

PROFILE

Dimensions of Wood Stock:
Body: 4″ long × 1½″ high × 1¼″ wide
Wings (2 pieces): 2½″ long × 1⅝″ wide × ¾″ thick

Eyes: 3mm dark brown or black
Actual length of live bird: 8″

TOP VIEW AND WINGS

FRONT VIEW

Plate 12

BLACKBURNIAN WARBLER

One of the most brilliantly colored birds of the East; once seen, the orange-and-black head of a male in breeding plumage will never be forgotten.

PROFILE

Dimensions of Wood Stock:
Body: 3½″ long × 1¼″ high × 1¼″ wide
Wings (2 pieces): 2½″ long × 1½″ wide × ½″ thick

Eyes: 2 or 3mm black or dark brown
Actual length of live bird: 5″

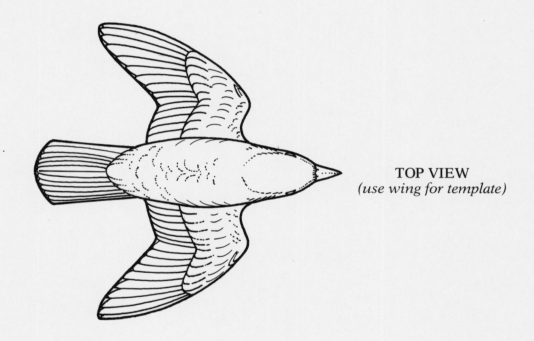

TOP VIEW
(use wing for template)

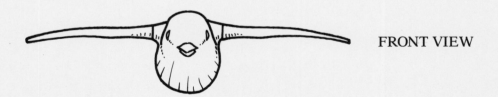

FRONT VIEW

Plate 13

RED-BREASTED NUTHATCH

*The most widespread of our nuthatches, frequently found in conifers. Like all its kin,
it can creep straight down as well as up a tree trunk.*

PROFILE

Dimensions of Wood Stock:
Body: 3½″ long × 1¼″ high × 1¼″ wide
Wings (2 pieces): 2½″ long × 1½″ wide ×
　½″ thick

Eyes: 2 or 3mm black or dark brown
Actual length of live bird: 4½″

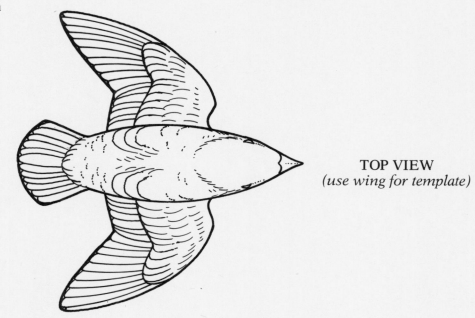

TOP VIEW
(use wing for template)

FRONT VIEW

Plate 14

RUBY-THROATED HUMMINGBIRD

*A welcome sight in warmer months, the Ruby-throat is the only
hummingbird ever seen in most of the East.*

PROFILE

Dimensions of Wood Stock:
Body (including tail): 2¾″ long × 1¼″ high
  × 1¼″ wide (tail may be cut from separate piece of stock and inserted into slot
  cut in body)
Bill: ⅛″ dowel or brass wire
Wings (2 pieces): 2¾″ long × 1″ wide ×
  ½″ thick

Eyes: 2mm black
Actual length of live bird: 3¾″

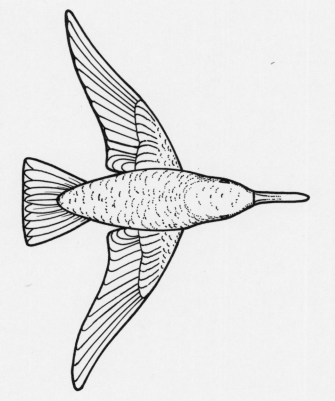

TOP VIEW
(use wing for template)

FRONT VIEW

Plate 15

ANNA'S HUMMINGBIRD

Increasingly common in much of the West, Anna's Hummingbird, unlike most of our hummingbirds, may be found over most of its range throughout the year.

PROFILE

Dimensions of Wood Stock:
Body (including tail): 3¼″ long × 1½″ high × 1¾″ wide (tail may be cut from separate piece of stock and inserted into slot in body)
Bill: ⅛″ dowel or brass wire
Wings (2 pieces): 3″ long × 1″ wide × ½″ thick

Eyes: 2mm black
Actual length of live bird: 4″

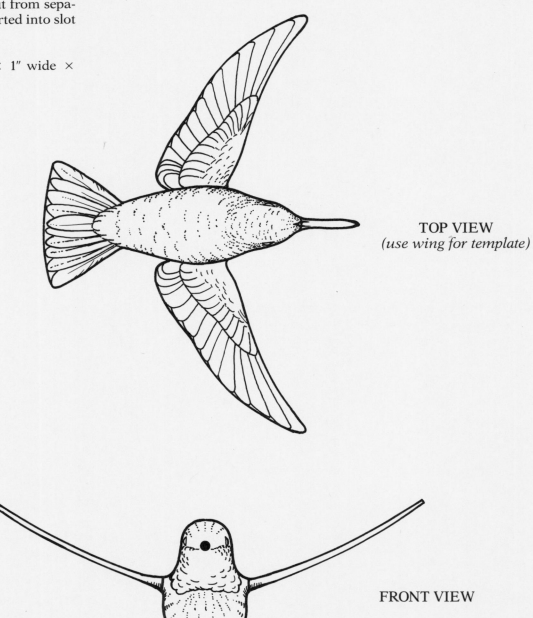

TOP VIEW
(use wing for template)

FRONT VIEW

Plate 16

to the secondaries and primaries. These feathers may then be indicated by first rough-notching with a sharp detailing knife, then sanding with very fine (#180 or finer) sandpaper. The method I prefer, however, is to use a wood-burning tool. For this kind of carving a chisel-shaped solid point on the burning tool works well. Don't forget to do the top and bottom surfaces of both wings. If you have never used a wood-burning tool before, see the section below titled "Burning In Feather Detail," where I give more information.

When you are satisfied with the appearance of both wings, you are ready to carve the body. Be sure that you have drawn a centerline all around the piece of wood (as shown in Fig. 3) and have traced the wing-joint surfaces on both sides of the body. Do not cut away any of these markings!

Now round out the head, referring to the patterns. Round the wood from the back of the neck to the front of the body and around the breast. To give the body a full look, carve carefully around the wing joints and slightly recess the body just under the wing joints. To represent the division of feathers into groupings on the back, use a small gouge to remove some wood in the area between the wings.

You are now ready to carve the body of the bird to conform fully to the shape of the patterns. Referring to the front-view pattern, taper around the breast from the bottom to the base of the head, working from the middle forward and then back along the body to the base of the tail. See also the top view. Remember not to cut away the centerline.

Next, concentrate again on the head. Notice that the lower part of a bird's head is wider than the top (see the front-view pattern). Keeping this in mind, taper the sides. This head width is now final and should be maintained to the end of your carving project. Study the patterns carefully and carve the bill. I have found that the best method is first to work from the top-view pattern to achieve the proper taper and then to finish carving the shape according to the profile. The tail should still remain unfinished at this point. It is a good idea to leave extra wood on the tail and any other thin, fragile areas until the rest of the basic carving has been completed, so as to avoid the likelihood of damaging potentially breakable parts.

At this stage you have yet to add the feather detail and the final shape of the tail. First check what you have carved so far. When you are satisfied that the shape of your carving is balanced and accurately conforms to the patterns, smooth away rough areas with a medium-grit sandpaper.

Now you can thin the tail. Working on the underside, use a small gouge and carve the tail down to a thickness of about 1/16". The entire body can now be sanded to a smooth finish with a fine grade of sandpaper (#220 or finer).

Next, if you intend to burn in feather detail, mark the body and tail feathers with a pencil, using the patterns and any other reference sources you have (such as photographs, drawings and field guides—the more the better) as guides. If you are using glass eyes (for which I have given sizes with the patterns), you should have drilled the eye holes by this time; if you have not, drill them now. A high-speed power drill with a proper-sized bit is the best

way to drill the eye sockets. On very small carvings such as these I prefer to emboss the eyes with a 3/32" nail set, and then paint them when I paint the body.

Check to make sure that you have marked the feathering as you wish. When you are satisfied, you are ready to join the wings to the body. The best method is as follows. In the wing-joint space on the body, push in a small, thin brass pin. Push it in at right angles to the body and at a point where, when the wing is joined to the body, the pin will not protrude through an outer surface of the wing. Leave about 3/16" of the pin exposed. Now, with wire cutters, clip off the head at an angle, to leave a sharp edge. Next, apply glue to both surfaces of the joint (on the body *and* wing), taking care not to use too much, and press the wing onto the body. Be sure the wing is aligned properly when you do this! Be ready to use a toothpick to wipe away any excess glue. I use yellow carpenter's glue for this procedure. Whichever type you use, *do not use a hot-melt glue* if you intend to burn in feather detail; the heat around the joint will remelt the glue and cause problems!

When the wings have been attached and the glue has dried you may proceed to adding feather detail by burning it in, as described immediately below. If you wish, this step may be skipped and the feathers and feather groupings simply painted on later.

Burning In Feather Detail

Considerable feather detail may be added by use of a wood-burning tool (pyroelectric pen). First be sure you are familiar with the use of the model you have purchased (they are available from woodcarving-supply outlets). You can practice on a piece of scrap wood of the type you are using for your carving. Before you begin, be sure that you have sketched in the feathers in as much detail as you wish to burn in. With practice you will be able to indicate at least the primary flight feathers and the tail feathers. Further practice will enable you to make your carving as realistically detailed as you wish.

A word of caution: be sure you have sanded your carving to a smooth finish *before* doing any wood burning. Sanding over wood-burned areas will undo much of your fine work as well as clogging the recesses around the feathers with wood dust.

Hanging the Carving

It is best to prepare your carving for hanging before you paint or otherwise finish it. The best way I have found to hang a miniature flying-bird carving is to drill a small hole all the way through from top to bottom at the balance point. Find this point by balancing the carving on a small, flat surface. I find the end of a 1/16" nail set just right for this. Let the carving fall slightly to one side or another, supporting it gently with your fingers, until you have found the point at which it will balance. Mark that point with a pencil. Next decide the angle at which you want the carving to hang and mark the appropriate point on the top of the carving. Have ready the string or other line you will use to hang the carving (I have found monofilament fishing line ideal for this purpose, since it is thin, strong, almost transparent and easy to handle). Between the two points you have marked drill a hole just slightly larger than the diameter of the string or line. My method for hanging the carving is to insert the monofilament so a small portion is protruding through the bottom (the breast area). Tie a double knot in this end and draw the monofilament back into the carving so the knot jams inside. (It may take practice to do this properly; if you start with an extra-long piece of monofilament you can always cut it down afterward.) When you have jammed the knot in the carving, tie a loop in the top end of the monofilament, of just the size and at just the height you want (see Fig. 5). Now you are ready to paint your carving and—the advantage of this method—you can hang it up to dry!

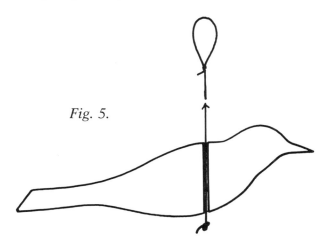

Fig. 5.

Finishing Your Carving

Generally the next step is to apply paint, but some hobbyists prefer to give their carvings a natural finish instead. If this is your intention, it is very important to give your work an extremely fine sanding (*before* wood burning!). Then, after sanding and any wood burning you may wish to do, apply varnish or shellac as desired. You may also consider staining the wood; just proceed as above and apply the stain before you apply the varnish or shellac. Remember to follow the instructions found on the labels of the products you use. Take special care to observe all safety precautions when working with volatile or toxic substances.

Most likely you will want to paint your carving in natural colors. To do so, prime it with three coats of gesso diluted to a thin wash. (Ordinary paint primer is satisfactory if your carving has little or no feather detail.) Allow for complete drying between coats. Once the wood has been thus coated, you are free to use sandpaper once more. It may be necessary to sand at this point if the primer raises the grain of the wood. If you do so, be sure to remove all of the resulting dust, or it may clog the feather detail. Now you are ready to paint your carving.

There are many different ways of painting wildlife carvings. What I offer here is a few basic procedures as an example. Before any actual painting, gather as many sources as you can that show the coloration of the species you are representing. Try to observe living birds whenever possible. This is not as difficult as it may sound. Many of the birds depicted in this book are frequent visitors to birdhouses and feeders. Even apartment-house dwellers in cities may be surprised at the variety and number of birds observable in nearby parks and open areas. I caution against just collecting photographs and other images without firsthand observation. Certain subtle aspects of form and color cannot be properly appreciated except in the living creatures themselves. Close study of these subtleties is therefore important, but it is also fun. With practice and observation, you will gradually find it becoming easier to paint realistically (naturally, that goes for carving as well).

The following procedures for painting the American Robin will give you an idea of how to paint any of the bird carvings in this book.

Always paint all of the larger areas of color before adding any detail. Since certain portions of this bird are white (see the color photograph on the inside cover), prime the entire carving with two coats of white paint (or three coats of gesso, as indicated above if you have burned-in or carved fine feather detail). Next, I strongly recommend marking in pencil the borders of the main areas of color. This will counteract a natural tendency to make the opposite sides of the carving dissimilar.

The back and upper portions of the head, wings and tail (except the two corner tail spots) should be painted with a mixture of black and white with a very small amount of burnt umber added. When the first coat has dried, add a bit more black to the mixture and use it to darken the crown, the wing primaries and the tail. Also mark the border of the throat and breast and add the dark streaks on the throat. Paint the underside of the primaries, secondaries and tail feathers with a medium-to-dark gray. The breast and flanks are of course Indian red. Paint the bill with cadmium yellow, medium. The under wing coverts and the area including the under tail coverts, behind the belly, as well as the corners of the tail, remain white. If you have painted over any of these white areas, repaint them with white now. This also holds true for the white area around the eyes. Mix some yellow ochre with Indian red to highlight feather edges on the breast.

Now carefully inspect your carving and repaint any thin or otherwise unsatisfactory areas. Even more detail may be added with a fine-tipped brush if you desire. Your ability to paint realistically will improve with practice and patience, and soon you will be able to give the feathers a look of fluffiness.

A Note on Suppliers

You may be able to buy such items as wood-burning tools, glass eyes and cast feet where you obtain your woodcarving and painting tools and materials. Check your local classified telephone directory. The following mail-order suppliers carry stocks of glass eyes and cast feet. It is a good idea to write or telephone for information before ordering.

Christian J. Hummul Co., Inc.
404 Brookletts Avenue
P.O. Box 1849
Easton, MD 21601
Telephone: (301) 820-8760

Ritter Carvers
William Ritter
1559 Dillon Road
Maple Glen, PA 19002
Telephone (after 5 P.M.): (215) 646-4896